Mammals of the High Mountain Ranges

Children's Science & Nature

BABY PROFESSOR
EDUCATION KIDS

Speedy Publishing LLC
40 E. Main St. #1156
Newark, DE 19711
www.speedypublishing.com

Copyright 2016

All Rights reserved. No part of this book may be reproduced or used in any way or form or by any means whether electronic or mechanical, this means that you cannot record or photocopy any material ideas or tips that are provided in this book

Mountains are interesting and beautiful. Some animals around the world prefer to live in the mountains. Although mountain habitats are more challenging because of the sudden change in temperatures, many animals, particularly mammals, still find themselves living in the mountain ranges.

In this book you meet some of the many mammals that live in high mountain ranges. Let's find out how they adapt to their constantly changing environment and how they survive.

In mountain habitats, animal species and weather rapidly change as elevation increases. However, despite the harsh climate, mountain ranges are still homes to diverse animals which have adapted to the changing environment.

Let's get to know the mammals that live in the mountain ranges. Many of these animals live in the lower altitudes for they find it hard to survive above the tree line because oxygen is scarce.

Gorillas

They live in the forests high in the African mountains. They can survive at elevations of 8,000 to 13,000 feet. Their thick fur helps them adapt and survive to their habitat with extremely low temperatures.

Pikas

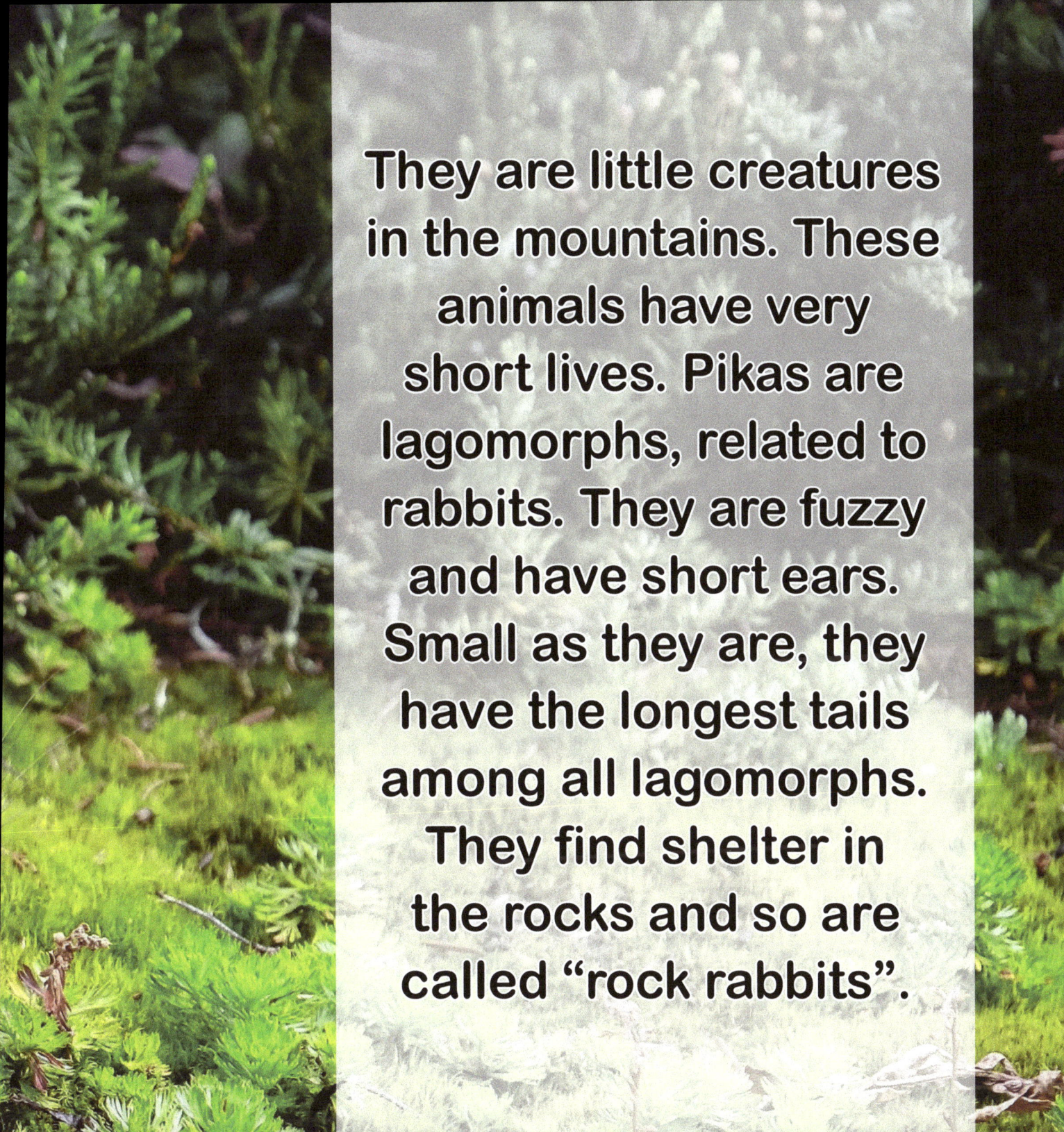

They are little creatures in the mountains. These animals have very short lives. Pikas are lagomorphs, related to rabbits. They are fuzzy and have short ears. Small as they are, they have the longest tails among all lagomorphs. They find shelter in the rocks and so are called "rock rabbits".

Bighorn Sheep

They are large mammals and are relatives of goats. The biggest threats to their lives are the tiny parasitic worms which live in their lungs. They are sure-footed animals and can easily move around the rugged mountain terrain. The males are called rams while the females are called ewes.

Elk

It is one of the largest species of deer in the world, and one of the largest mammals in North America and eastern Asia. They are herbivores, which means that they feed on grass, bushes and saplings. They are great runners and swimmers because of their long and powerful legs.

Rocky Mountain Goats

These mountain animals spend most of their time in the rocky, barren land above the tree line. They do not hibernate, migrate or live under ground or in snow banks. They are considered as the most sure-footed of all mountain animals. With their four stomachs, they forage and digest a large volume of plants every day. Their woolly undercoat and long shaggy outercoat protect them from extreme cold.

Squirrels

They deal with the harsh cold of winter by hibernating. Squirrels look for underground burrows and sleep there for months. When they hibernate, their body temperature stays around 45 to 50 degrees Fahrenheit.

Ibexes

These are wild goats. They are found in the mountainous regions of Europe, north central Asia and Northern Africa. These animals are a relative of antelopes, buffalo, bison, cattle, goats and sheep. They possess long, curved horns and cloven hooves.

These warm blooded animals have developed ways to deal with the harsh conditions in the mountains. They hibernate, migrate or seek protection under ground or under the snow. Many mountain habitats have been protected because they are prone to destruction and degradation despite their inaccessibility. They are still a haven to some endangered animal species around the world.

Lightning Source UK Ltd.
Milton Keynes UK
UKHW050749260922
409435UK00006B/6

Printed in Dunstable, United Kingdom

Where Love Begins

Look out for the sequel, *Where Love Begins*, out now!

As Angela and Jay settle into their new life together in New York City, they're determined to build a future while helping to mend the broken ties with her family. But just as they start to find their footing, unexpected challenges and shocking revelations threaten to pull them apart.

Meanwhile, Isabella embarks on a personal mission to heal the wounds of her past and recover what she lost long ago—her son. Returning to her village in Sicily, she's faced with the heartbreaking consequences of leaving and vows to make amends for her mistakes.

Where one journey ends, another one begins. Join Angela and Isabella on an unforgettable journey of love, redemption, and the search for the one thing that matters most—family. *Where Love Begins* will have you hooked from the very first page.

embrace felt distant, like a bad dream. Angela clung to her father, her body still trembling, tears streaming down her cheeks.

Suddenly, she felt another pair of arms wrap around her and her father, pulling them both into a tight embrace. Through her blurred vision, she saw him—Jay. He was sobbing, his face pale, but his eyes full of relief. He pressed his lips to her cheek, his voice hoarse with emotion. "I thought I'd lost you. I thought you were gone."

Angela buried her face in his chest, her hands gripping his shirt. The fear, the tension, all the horror of the last hour began to unravel as she felt his warmth, his presence. She pulled back just enough to look into his tear-filled brown eyes, the love and fear swirling in them overwhelming her. Jay kissed her softly, his lips lingering on her forehead. "I'm never letting you go," he whispered back, holding her tightly as if to anchor them both in the storm that had almost torn them apart.

For the first time in what felt like forever, Angela felt a flicker of hope, a light in the darkness. Whatever came next, she knew one thing for certain—Jay was her constant, her truth in a world full of lies. Just when she thought her life was crumbling around her and love was ending, she realised, this was where love begins.

"I'm not going anywhere," she whispered, her voice choked with tears. "I'm never losing you, Jay. Not ever."

Four simultaneous shots rang out, the sharp crack of gunfire cutting through the tense silence. Marco's body jerked violently as the bullets ripped through him—one piercing his skull, another tearing into his chest, and the other two hitting his legs. His eyes went wide, blood splattering across the floor.

Angela's breath caught in her throat as she saw his already lifeless body begin to fall toward her, his large frame collapsing like a toppled statue. Panic surged through her, her limbs frozen in shock. Her mother leapt forward, throwing herself on top of Angela, shielding her as Marco's dead weight came crashing down.

The next few moments were a blur.

Police officers swarmed the café from every direction, shouting commands, their boots thudding against the ground. Isabella clung to Angela, sobbing uncontrollably as she wrapped her arms protectively around her daughter's trembling body and pressed a gentle kiss to her forehead. An officer grabbed Isabella, pulling her to safety, but Angela couldn't move—she couldn't breathe. The scene before her was too much, too surreal. Marco's lifeless form lay crumpled on the floor, blood pooling beneath him.

Daniel broke free from an officer's grasp and rushed toward Angela, his face pale with shock. "Angela!" he shouted, his voice thick with emotion as he pulled her into his arms. "I'm sorry, darling. I'm so, so sorry." His tears soaked into her hair as he held her tight, his body shaking with sobs. "I'll make this right, I promise. I'll never let anything happen to you again."

He held her as though she might slip away, his words a desperate mantra of regret and guilt. The world outside the

167